IT'S AN
ILL WIND

IT'S AN ILL WIND

The Adventures of Rip Rasper through the
World of Farting

Written and Illustrated
by
DERMOT HYDE

'The rumbling of a fart or any sound,
Is only air reverberating round.'
(*Chaucer*)

MICHAEL JOSEPH
London

MICHAEL JOSEPH
Published by the Penguin Group
27 Wrights Lane, London W8 5TZ, England
Viking Penguin Inc., 40 West 23rd Street, New York 10010, USA
Penguin Books Australia Ltd, Ringwood, Victoria, Australia
Penguin Books Canada Ltd, 2801 John Street, Markham, Ontario, Canada L3R 1B4
Penguin Books (NZ) Ltd, 182–190 Wairau Road, Auckland 10, New Zealand

Penguin Books Ltd, Registered Offices: Harmondsworth, Middlesex, England

First published in 1989

Typeset in Linotron 11 on 13 pt Clearface Regular
by Goodfellow and Egan Cambridge Ltd

Printed and bound in Italy by L.E.G.O. – Vicenza

A CIP catalogue record for this book is available
from the British Library

ISBN 0 7181 3312 9

CONTENTS

Come lusty companions and lift off with me,
Feel hearty and welcome in my company,
Your servant and guide till our ways they do part,
Rip Rasper's the name – all aboard then, let's start!

THEREBY HANGS A 'TALE'

The complete story of farting has never appeared on paper, and certainly not in the English language. Most great writers, it seems, never really felt free to 'vent' their 'scent'-iments on this 'fundamental' area of human relations. In today's nuclear age, do we appreciate, for example, that wars and revolutions in the past have actually been sparked off by the less than diplomatic unleashing of a fetid fart under the wrong circumstances?

How many readers would believe that in our grandfathers' day several continental cities could boast their own professional farters, all of whom took their respective music-hall audiences by storm? Who would believe that 200 years ago child genius Mozart would have found time to address himself to this most musically harmonious of subjects? Even the headstrong Romans worshipped a God of Farting – the almighty Crepitus! Shocked? There's more to come!

The author has ruthlessly followed the 'rip-roaring scent' of the fart down through the annals of history from the 'crack' of dawn up to the computer-age. He has pursued the trail of an hilarious and horrific pastime bound to delight the noses and ears of both young and old alike. He has examined the nature and appearance of the fart as he wends his way through the history books, expressing himself in both cultural and scientific form. Just how the inhibited fart, 'under pressure' in a hostile society, has managed to survive until the present day, is told with the help of anecdotes, poems, prophesies and predictions.

The author's search for information relating to the subject was not an easy one. Most major newspapers and periodicals were too embarrassed to print his cries of help for material. Despite this, a vast amount of information was made available and the author would like to thank all those who contributed so generously. Finally, the following chapters are dedicated to those unfortunate souls who genuinely appreciate the breaking of wind backwards, but just haven't got the 'guts' to do it!

CLEARING THE AIR

or

Farting and Farts

Who knows what it is then, a fart?
It's a breeze that's just trying to be smart.
But timid or loud
This strange little cloud,
Is so sad and so loathe to depart.

In some respects, Rip Rasper almost defies definition. One philosopher described him as a 'failed attempt to make your backside speak'. At times he was treated as a taboo subject, at others raised to the level of an art form. Regarded by some as a natural process, by others as an acoustic phenomenon, Rip's status has changed according to circumstances.

Apart from his acute sense of smell, the most important quality possessed by our little friend is his highly developed power of speech. Like humans, Rip Rasper is capable of expressing loud aggressive dominance or quiet seductive persuasion – sometimes he prefers just to waft around without uttering a word!

His relationship with human beings is a tenuous one. On

entering our world he assumes the role of a traveller with no fixed abode, trying to make the most of his short time amongst us. Almost like a zealous Christian missionary, his job is to get to know as many of us as possible in the short span of time allotted. Rich, poor, strong or weak, to Rip Rasper all men are equal.

To Rip Rasper all men are equal

Like most of the human population the fart population is made up of loud-mouths – 'Crepitus' as the Romans called them – and quieter types – 'Flatus' types. Beware, both kinds can prove dangerous!

A sure way of losing all your friends within seconds is to allow a pungent Crepitus to pay a visit. On the other hand, should the dastardly fiend decide to leave his aroma at home he can still prove humorous in breaking the ice at parties. A pungent sneaky Flatus, however, should never be ignored, for, being

8

noiseless, all his energy is invested in the rotten stench he creates. Because he is silent it is a continual source of argument as to who exactly fathered him – in short, he's a bastard!

> *I'm Rip and to find out my status,*
> *It's so simple, there's no apparatus.*
> *From the sound and the smell*
> *It's so easy to tell,*
> *If not Crepitus, I must be a Flatus.*

Enough hot air, let's take this opportunity and ask Rip to introduce us to a few of his friends and relations:

HURRICANE HORACE (or The Military Fart)

Hi there! I'm Rip's cousin and usually a Flatus-with-aroma type emitted by soldiers indoors. I'm often deliberately released by senior military in an attempt to test the mettle of the younger lads. The best approach is to pay no heed to me whatsoever. Occurring outdoors, try marching slightly out of time in order to break down the density of my smell.

GREAT-UNCLE DR BLOW
(or The Academic Fart)

Good day. I'm no chicken, I know, but I'm full of 'guts', I'll tell you. I usually rely on my volume for good results, so I'm discharged openly and often accompanied by loud laughter in the classroom. Let me run loose for there is nothing you can do to prevent my movement. Great revelry and screaming are the first reactions and it is only a question of time until the teacher has lost control of the class. Everyone should accuse each other of having unloaded the detonation as this wastes even more of the class time.

9

THE FASHIONABLE FART

Probably the most common emission of all, he inevitably blows his ugly horn in mixed company. To avoid a disaster, check whether he is travelling with a strong aroma. If the answer is positive:

1: head for the main exit (difficult as it is usually too late);
2: even if it is the host sitting next to you, blame him or her for the offence!
3: whether smoker or not, light a pipe using the strongest smelling tobacco you can lay hands on in order to cover the hideous scent deposited by your back-passage;
4: allow yourself to be forcibly ejected!

Should your anal offering be without-aroma but nevertheless rather deafening then:

1: cough or sneeze loudly at the same time as evacuating the culprit (this takes years of practise);
2: ignoring what has happened, rise and change seats, distancing yourself from this 'foul' event;
3: whilst farting, shout loudly acknowledging the presence of someone as if you hadn't seen them for years (whereas you both travelled down in the same bus about twenty minutes before).

Remember! Whatever type your backside breeze turns out to be, there is no point in *not* allowing him to escape – as Salvador Dali warned us:

'It is better to fart in company than to die alone in the corner.'
(*Diary of a Genius*)

10

THE SPITFIRE

Due to his sheer volume, 'The Spitfire' is guaranteed to rudely awaken at least 50% of those asleep in the army barracks. A particularly deafening delivery, he causes immediate panic forcing the occupants to rise and dress themselves rapidly. You, as the culprit, must also rise and dress otherwise you are instantly recognised as the 'arsonist'.

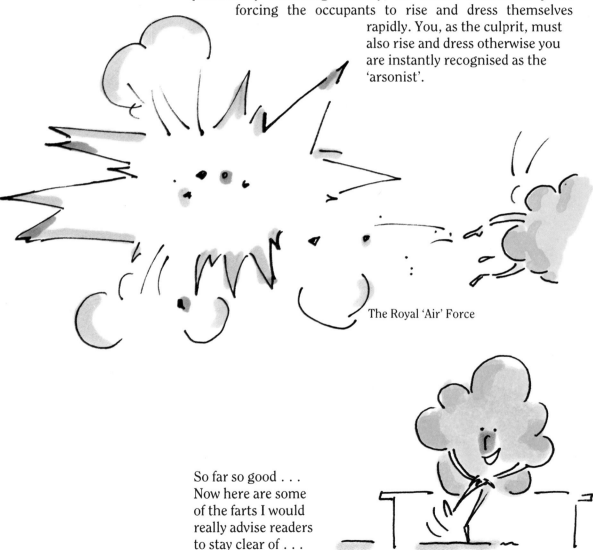

The Royal 'Air' Force

So far so good . . .
Now here are some
of the farts I would
really advise readers
to stay clear of . . .

THE HOG

Thankfully no relation of Rip Rasper's, this guy needs no introduction. A flexible chap, he seems to vary whenever we vary our diet. Normally we are more than relieved when he is discharged, for he has probably been the cause of indigestion or some other uncomfortable rumblings. No excuses are required as he has become an accepted part of our daily lives.

HI FOLKS!

THE SQUID

Has been described as being 'like a bunny in his burrow that doesn't know which hole to come out of'. An indecisive consignment, he may, if in a moody disposition, simply crawl his way back to the bowel and remain there as if nothing had happened. Safely ensconced there, he is normally prepared to bide his time – all night if necessary. Should he decide to make for the exit, he must be stifled as soon as possible by tight clenching of the buttock muscles and forced back into the intestine. Be prepared to take the consequences which are:

    1: a gigantic great burp, or
    2: a hellishly loud rumbling in your gut, or
    3: terrible pains in the stomach and lower abdomen.

All of these are surely preferable to the smell and the noise which would otherwise have been created!

THE BULLOCK

Always a loud belligerent offering, he is disgorged by those who indulge in regular sporting activities or those who are otherwise silly enough to subject themselves to regular physical stress. Tensed-up buttock muscles contribute considerably towards the incredible sound quality.

12

THE WATER-BUFFALO (or The Liquidiser)

Sometimes referred to as a 'Wet Fart', this parcel of tricks arouses great fear because, depending upon the chemistry of the bowel at the particular time, one can never be certain as to what form the accompanying deposit may take. In this case it is not only sound and smell which are the decisive factors, for once the floodgates have been opened, the optical side and its after-effects can cause severe problems for the host and her furniture. Be careful, it could be your last excitable!!!

Lull Before the Storm

THE SKUNK (or The Spoilsport)

The theatre and the concert hall are his favourite hiding places, and if cornered there one is powerless – no escape! He is usually of the sneaky Flatus variety, and to avoid coming 'nose to nose' with him, the best advice is to restrict your cultural lifestyle.

THE JACKASS (or The Ladylike)

Feel free to snigger and laugh if you encounter him. With a noise like a high-pitched bird, he is at home in cafés, Women's Institutes, in fact everywhere where women congregate in any numbers. On hearing him have no inhibitions in playfully chastising your neighbour's buttocks, thus engaging her in much awaited conversation.

Complicated, isn't it? As you can see there are many types of fart from which to choose. Readers should seek out the type of emission best suited to the occasion and their own mood at that time. Feel free to 'break new wind' by trying your hand at an 'effart' of your very own.

Here's a few more to whet your appetite:

THE ADMINISTRATIVE (or The Pen-pusher).

A big 'hit' with civil-servants and Gas Board employees.

THE PROVINCIAL

Very much at home amongst the farming community and landed gentry in and around the Lumbar Regions.

THE BULLY

Popular amongst sales representatives and others whose internal organs require urgent medical attention.

THE YUPPIE

The cause of many a financial 'windfall' on the stock exchange, he is also renowned for 'blowing' up a storm in social circles.

THE SPORT OF KINGS

or

Farting and Sport

That big race from Stoke to Carlisle,
Where young Rip broke the two-minute mile,
Sure the blast of his rear
Blew him on to Tangier,
So he's given up sport for a while.

Games and sports involving farting go back several thousand years, and the most popular of all pastimes was the extinguishing of candles by farting them out. Even at the turn of this century there were a few professional farters who managed to make quite a good living at their 'sport', and one of the greatest farting sportsmen of all time was Josef Pujol, better known as *Le Petomane*. Pujol blew the house down (and the candles out) everywhere he appeared. At the turn of the century there was no one in the same league as this maestro.

As everyone knows, sport can damage your health, but what many people do not know is that excessive farting can also damage your sport!

Rip Rasper went weak at the knees,
As he raced down the Alps on his skis,
The avalanche that started,
Just after he'd farted,
Could be heard to the far Pyrenees.

Compared with skiing where the skier has no one but himself to blame, horse-racing seems to be the ideal sport for would-be-farters — the idea being that the horses themselves, whilst jumping over so many obstacles, are made responsible for the tremendous blastings. Sensible riders, be they six-stone jockeys or 22-stone slobs, should avail themselves of the opportunity to release all this unwanted energy. Nevertheless, to rule out the chances of a horse and jockey farting all through a race and gaining the unfair advantage of being thrust towards the finishing post with each successive fart, organisers are today considering pre-race checks on the diets of both horses and riders. In the near future success at Epsom in the 3.30 Handicap may depend more on the size and nature of the jockey's bowels than upon his sporting ability!

Football, of course, cannot be left out of the farting scene. Unlike horse-racing where the animal can be blamed, the footballer faces a more frustrating situation with a massive crowd breathing in, and listening to, his every noise and smell. However, not all spectators seem insulted by the odd pungent puff from a footballer's nether regions, even if he happens to be an amateur like Rip Rasper:

It's not easy young Rip to dishearten,
But it's sure from his club he'll be partin',
He's no time to score goals,
For he's off blowin' holes,
The crowd love to see our Rip fartin'.

'Bottoms Up!'

It is, of course, in the pub that the real Farting Olympics take place. It is here that the truly professional sporting farter will squeeze his body to the utmost limits. Surrounded by gallons of drink and a selection of his favourite pub games our sedentary red-nosed gladiator is in his element. Of course he thinks nothing of spilling yet another pint of bitter over his friends engaged in a heated game of 'draughts' (or was it 'back'-gammon?), as he lets fly a couple of award-winning backside darts. Because it would involve parting with his beer glass for the duration of the game, it goes without saying that activities such as ping-'pong' will probably never really attract such beer-swilling sporties.

Jogging to and from the pub (particularly to it), has also become a popular activity amongst many controversial athletes in recent years. In fact, many of the serious keep-fit community take this practice so seriously they can be seen (providing visibility is good) attempting to gallop home from the pub after 17 pints of Guinness in rhythm to their own farting. A truly admirable sporting achievement not without its health dangers, this strange sporting activity apparently demands more co-ordinational talent than is required to fly Concorde – a sobering thought indeed!

More aggressive and physical sports such as wrestling and judo, with combatants locked informally together for relatively long periods of time, can quickly lead to frayed nerves and excitable bowels. The frustration and annoyance can eventually prove too much to 'bare' whenever, in the middle of a competition, an opponent's colon decides to speak its mind; consideration should be given to the introduction of the robust non-toxic anal muzzles at present in use in Scandinavian countries. Unfortunately, in this country, where competitors are not yet forced to wear rear-end catalysators by law, many a Black Belt maestro has been demoted to Brown Belt mediocrity within seconds!!

The Knock-Out 'Blow'

Finally, when it comes to competitive spirit in the field of farting there is no one can 'blow their horn' better than the ladies, especially when they are amongst themselves. Consider the amount of 'hot air' released during the following 'long-winded' outrageous event:

19

THE FARTING COMPETITION

Now here is a ditty that's certain to please
Of a grand farting contest at Stockton-on-Pease,
Where all the best arses parade on the field
To enter the contest for various shields.

Some lift up their arses and fart up the scale
To compete for a cup or a barrel of ale,
While others, whose arses are biggest and strongest,
Compete in a contest of loudest and longest.

Now this Easter evening had drawn a great crowd
And the betting was even on Mrs McCleod,
For 'twas written in papers of latest edition
That this lady's arse was in perfect condition.

And young Mrs Brown was backed for a place
As she'd always been placed in the deepest disgrace,
For dropping a fart that drowned the church organ
And gassing the verger, poor Mr Morgan.

But old Mrs Jones had a perfect backside
With a bunch of black hair and a wart on each side,
And she fancied her chance of winning with ease
Having trained on a diet of cabbage and peas.

Mrs Bugle arrived amidst roars of applause
And promptly proceeded to pull down her drawers,
For although she'd no chance in this farting display
'Twas the best arse that I'd seen for many a day.

The judges arrived and ascended the stand
And began to address this remarkable band:
'This contest is on, as said on the bills,
We've forbidden the use of injections or pills.'

The ladies lined up at a signal to start
And winning the toss Mrs Jones took first fart,
The crowd stood amazed in such silence and wonder
The BBC news announced warnings of thunder.

Then Mrs Porthole was called to the front
And started by doing a marvellous stunt.
With well bunched-up cheeks and tightly clenched hands
She farted the roof off the sixpenny stands.

But young Mrs Brown thought nothing of this
For she'd drunk weak tea, and was all wind and piss.
She took up her stance with legs opened wide
But unluckily shat, and was disqualified.

Next came Mrs Bugle who shyly appeared
And smiled to the crowd as they lustily cheered,
For though it was thought that her chances were small
She beat the whole lot, and out-farted them all.

She stood at the front where she farted alone
And the crowds were amazed at the sweetness of tone.
The judges agreed without hindrance or pause:
'First prize, Mrs Bugle. Pull up your drawers.'

She walked to the rostrum with maidenly gait
To receive from the vicar a set of gold plate,
And turned to the crowd as they started to sing,
And farted the last verse of God Save the King.

BEASTLY PRACTICES

or

Farting and Animals

Said a snail to young Rip most irate,
'It's your smell that we animals hate,
It's no joke to be gassed,
To be breathing your last,
And to end up on somebody's plate.'

The donkey is without doubt the king of farters in the animal world, and in almost every language his ability to bray discordantly via his back-passage is praised and admired. If insulting a person of a lower background, one refers to him as 'having been farted against the wall by a donkey'. A freckly-faced

23

person may be described as having been 'farted in the face by a donkey'. A womaniser or flatterer is described by the fair sex as one who is 'as full of compliments as a donkey is full of farts'. Politicians praise each other's ability to mislead their public when they, 'twist their words like a donkey its fart'.

In the Soviet Union however, since the world has got 'wind' of *glasnost*, the donkey no longer reigns as farting king and Mr Gorbachov has replaced him with, believe it or not, the pigeon. Interestingly enough, the Soviet reasoning behind this controversial decision is based upon traditional Russian religious beliefs:

The Russians are cruel and unfair,
For the donkey they don't seem to care,
They allow no religion,
For their god is the pigeon,
Who can fart where he likes in Red Square.

Strangely, the oldest reference we have concerning animals farting makes no reference at all to our star exhibitionist the donkey. Instead, two lesser known 'B' factors the Bull and the Buck take the lead roles in a work written over 700 years ago in 1250 called 'The Cuckoo Song'. Their waking hours seem to have been spent leaping around and discharging from the rear the entire day long:

'*Bulluc sterteth, buck ferteth*' – a formidable duo indeed!

But bucks and bulls are in no way allowed to 'hog' the stage in the animal world of farting. A lover of all creatures great and small, Rip Rasper sides with no one when it comes to pronouncing on windy beasts. Quietly confident, Rip is justifiably proud of the mental ability displayed by his own 17-year-old pet cow Smudge.

'My cow farts more intelligently than you speak.'

Being a close relation of the donkey, it comes as no surprise that the horse too can hold his own as a farter, and is in fact probably the most musical farter in the animal kingdom – or so we are told by the long-winded French writer Rabelais, who tells us his hero Panurge

> would fart like a horse, and the women would laugh and say, How now do you fart Panurge? No no, Madam (said he), I do but tune my tail to the plain song of the Musick, which you make with your nose.

If horses prove to be gifted musical farters, why then have none of their inbred talents rubbed off on their nearest relatives, the donkey and the ass? The musical ability of these two amateurs appears to be more than suspect:

Who's more talented, the ass or the donkey?
When they fart they're both in the wrong key.
I don't think it's the latter,
For the windows they shatter,
'Cos the pitch and the tuning's all wonky.

Even when they are dead, the reputations of the donkey and the ass take some beating. Consider this description of a despairing man:

> In the Name of God: I had rather undertake the fetching of a Fart forth of the Belly of a dead Ass, then to draw out of you a positive and determinate Resolution.

During the Middle Ages superstition had it, should a man's horse fart three times in succession the owner would die within 24 hours. In 'hindsight' and considering the power 'behind' some large beasts, it would be surprising if a victim would last anything like 24 hours after the 'death-blow' had been struck. But even if a human being should happen to lose his life as a result of an animal farting, Rip Rasper still urges us to respect the sensitivity of all animals should nature force them to 'fowl' the air in our presence – after all they are only human!

Keep calm and head straight for the priest
When a fart has been let by a beast.
Don't scold or chastise
Or the animal despise
Keep still and respect the deceased.

Strange to say, few people lose their lives nowadays as a result of beastly blow-outs, in fact all too often the opposite is the case. The situation where an innocent dog or goldfish is blamed for his master's shallow gutless explosions is common and any naïve pet will serve to allow the real culprit to save face . . .

'Very Fishy'

To be fair, human beings farting in the presence of animals is something which should be avoided. The following inclement treatment meted out to an unfortunate fox by a so-called 'Lady' really does leave much to be desired – once again the French writer Rabelais reports:

> But the false old trot did so fistle and fist, that she stunk like a hundred devils, which put the poor fox to a great deal of ill-ease, for he knew not to what side to turn himself, to escape the unsavoury perfume of this old woman's postern blasts.

Sadly, treatment of this kind is not confined to foxes. When visitors arrive, how often has father shown a sudden interest in taking Rover the dog for a walk, only with the intention of releasing his own gaseous rear-end gales in the open air? Unfortunately Rover is forced to accept his master's unfair treatment and escape is impossible if he happens to be on a lead. Were the tables to be turned, with Rover in the driving 'seat' – where is the dog-owner who would not 'end up' chastising his poor pet's buttocks?

Said Rover out walking one day,
'It's time that we dogs had a say,'
So he blasted and gusted,
His arse upward thrusted,
And now he's been sold as a stray.

28

Perhaps human beings could learn a lesson from animals when it comes to farting. Beasts certainly vent as much as we do but it seems there is no social stigma or taboo attached to the activity in animal circles. When guests are invited to dinner and Rover the dog lying sprawled in front of the fireplace suddenly lets loose a giddy gas from his rear, surely no apology is necessary in a civilised society?

In short, we still have a long way to go when it comes to respecting the farts of animals, for it seems there are no limits to the length unscrupulous individuals will go in order to abuse and embarrass the animal population. Sadly, well-respected intellectuals must also share the blame. That unashamed writer Jonathan Swift, for example, even went so far as to suggest the possibility of earning ourselves much needed pocket-money by taking advantage of poor defenceless donkeys in the following manner:

Extracting farts from a dead donkey and selling them at five pence a yard

Where are the animal lovers amongst us who are prepared to entertain such 'beastly practices?' Sadly, the Royal Society for the Prevention of Cruelty to Animals is unable to cope with the situation. In order to protect our animals (especially abused donkeys), more financial support is required and informed experts advocate the world-wide expansion of new organisations such as 'ILLWIND' the Institute for Legalising the Liberation of Winds Induced in Nags and Donkeys. Is Royalty prepared to help strike a 'blow' for animal liberation? The time for nagging is past, so let us put our money where our nose-bag should be and show our support for RIP RASPER'S ILLWIND APPEAL!

FOOD FOR THOUGHT

or

Farting and Food

On Holiday in old London town
Rip would blast on his head like a clown,
He'd eat lots of meat,
So the smell was more sweet,
As he hung from Tower Bridge upside down.

Although fartologists the world over do not agree on all the reasons why human beings fart so much, they are united on one point at least – without food we would probably not be able to fart at all! It seems our ability to let rip depends more on the type and quality of food we eat rather than on the quantity.

But it all goes in one end and comes out the other, so what's the problem?

Well it's not quite that simple! Just how important food is for our 'fartability' is explained in the August 1974 edition of *World Medicine* where the earnestness of the situation is cited quite plainly for all to 'digest':

> The lower gut is just like an industrial fermentation tank, whose gaseous contents can be varied with infinite delicacy by nutrient changes, exploded by a spark at the wrong moment, or discharged dramatically in a blowout. A slight dietary change and you can have sweetness instead of light!

32

In other words, beware of what you eat, for as we shall see, some foodstuffs are more risky than others.

Many types of vegetable can prove hazardous, such as peas; but peas are not the only culprit and beans must be apportioned an even greater share of the blame. The havoc beans wreck on the defenceless human bowel is a medical tragedy. The famous scientist Dr H. Buttes writing in 1599 regarding the consumption of beans as downright immoral. In his work *Dyets Drie Dinner* he bellowed:

'Others referre it to beans flatulence, whereby they provoke to *lechery.*'

A Little Tit-Bit

One hopes the Directors of Heinz Beans are aware of the flatulence as well as the sexual prowess of most of their customers! But beans not only make you explode, they make you explode loudly even if you happen to be old and disabled:

Said the doc to a man with a hump,
'You've a problem just down by your rump,
        Try eating some greens
        Give up the old beans
For your blasting makes everyone jump.'

33

Along with beans, chilli is as good a foodstuff as any with which to damage our insides permanently, as Rip Rasper's young companion Master William found out to his cost:

> It's Rip's friend, the dopey wee Willie,
> He's injured himself, he's so silly.
> Now his backside it's burst,
> But he must be the first,
> To get brain damage eating hot chilli.

Brain damage due to eating 'windy victuals' is not as uncommon an ailment as it would seem. Rabelais warns us to be careful with certain foodstuffs as they are liable to cause farting and thus lower our IQ!!

> You are likewise to abstain from Beans, as also from Coleworts, Cabbage, and all other such windy victuals which may endanger the troubling of your brains, and the dimming or casting a kind of mist over your animal spirits.

So what can we eat without stinking and blowing the place to pieces?

In general, foodstuffs containing carbohydrates prove risky for most farters. Any carbohydrates not absorbed by the intestine receive a good 'going-over' from surrounding bacteria and those are the fellows that produce unsavory stenches. Beans, for example, contain a lot of carbohydrates which are not absorbed due to lack of enzymes. Heavy consumption of beans, therefore, is a 'sound' way of losing a lot of friends. One solution is to dispatch the foul winds in another direction and spices which would help us to belch more and fart less include ginger, nutmeg and cinnamon. After consuming any of these the air produced normally tends to drift in an upward direction, so it's a question of deciding on the lesser of two evils!

But is it evil to fart? Of course not – on the contrary! In the 16th century musky grunting via the back passage after a meal was the 'in' thing and normally displayed a gesture of thanks towards the host – in fact, not to indulge was positive bad manners. If after one of his banquets Martin Luther got no response from his guests he would inashamedly ask of his company:

'Why is it that no one does belch or does fart,
    If the food was that bad, well then why did ye start?'

Should his esteemed guests still insist upon keeping their 'fowl' 'gas'tronomical wise-'cracks' to themselves, Luther would encourage them just a little further.

'Try burping and farting it's never too late,
Was it not to your liking the food that you ate?'

The Ancient Egyptians went even further in their praise for farting and were prepared to elevate garlic, for example, to the level of a god simply because it possessed the power to make one fart. The resulting winds were said to be divine.

An East Indian tribe, the Tamula, has a strange custom in connection with the wedding ceremony in this respect. As soon as the bride becomes engaged all the relations are invited to her house for a feast and all the visitors bring various cereals with them. It's the happy couple's task to eat as much of the cereal as possible and as it is all fairly flatulent stuff both are soon gusting the place out. If their spicy breezes are insufficient or

35

simply not loud enough, the relatives insist that the boy does not proceed with the ceremony as it would augur ill for the future. If, on the other hand, the relations are satisfied with the gassy performance, the son may marry and he receives a handsome dowry to take with him into the marriage.

In Ancient Egypt garlic was elevated to the level of a god

Quite in contrast to this, a belief prevalent among many of the Roman nobility was that the consumption of more than one large fish before midday would lead to severe bowel eruptions and be regarded as a bad omen. The foul heavy air prevailing that Ides of March when Caesar was murdered was probably no exception. It was little wonder that poor old Brutus lost his head with smelly Julius.

Even if the human body has become used to a certain diet, a sharp change in circumstances, geographical or otherwise, can have disastrous results. Several years ago, a Japanese diving

End of story – 'end' of Caesar!

team travelled to the shores of Loch Ness in the Scottish Highlands in search of the monster Nessie. Knowing the poor reputation of Scottish and indeed British fare, the Japs decided to bring their own supplies of spiced tripe and Tokyo Onions with them. After several weeks the visitors were refused admittance to the public conveniences in the area due to the obnoxious odours their food produced after consumption. The locals were 'aghassed'. The Nips returned to the 'land of the rising sun' without sighting Nessie, but one relic of their sojourn in the area still remains to this day. The following verse penned by the locals and erected near the spot where the Japs set up camp commemorates their venture:

Thank God, that's the last o' the Japs,
Their visit was full o' mishaps,
For while huntin' old Nessie
They farted so messy
Noo oor shops are sold oot o' jockstraps!

The famous Greek philosopher Hippocrates recognised the harmless connection between food, drink and farting in the following way:

> All food and drink contains the spirit of the world. As you eat you take this spirit into your body; this is proved by the fact that after eating, you expel air from the body. Air of this sort is merely an excess of spirit.

Hippocrates the 'Hippocrite'! 'An excess of spirit' indeed!

Talking of spirits, drink in all its forms proves a very able contender for the trophy 'Fart Producer No 1' of all time. During the Middle Ages when they really enjoyed slurping their plonk in Merrie Olde England, unfortunate boozers had to suffer continual harassment in the form of harsh warnings such as the following:

Such wines engender a masse of many crudities and much
flatuouesness!
(*Surflet: Countrie Farm, 1605*)

So getting drunk and releasing a jolly good rat-a-tat from the
rear is nothing new – they were hard at it even in the 14th
century as Geoffrey Chaucer depicts in the following idyllic
scene of family life:

> *That was the lot; no sleeping-draught was needed.*
> *The miller had taken so much booze unheeded,*
> *He snorted like a cart-horse in his sleep*
> *And vented other noises, loud and deep.*
> *His wife joined in the chorus hot and strong;*
> *Two furlongs off you might have heard their song.*
>
> The Reeve's Tale

But it's not just cheap wine that creates raucous bellowing from
behind, for even the most expensive champagne can also
produce the goods! Sadly however, Rip Rasper was just one
among many who was forced to learn this fact the hard way:

> *Rip Rasper's been at it again.*
> *For weeks he's been guzzling champagne,*
> *Said his friends, 'You'll get better,*
> *Just slip off your sweater,*
> *And fart, take the weight off your brain.'*

39

We must remember that after either eating or drinking the evacuation of air from our gut is a perfectly normal and natural activity and it should certainly not be suppressed.

True as this may be, I'm afraid, Mrs McGurk would take an awful lot of convincing! Her husband Victor ('Victor the Venter' to his workmates) had attended the office party and swallowed 17 pints of Guinness. So as not to waken the wife, he tiptoed inside the door at three o'clock in the morning. As he closed the door quietly behind himself, the cuckoo-clock struck loudly three times. Cursing to himself, McGurk was sure the wife had heard everything by now. Tomorrow he'd be for the high jump! In an effort to rescue the situation he himself cuckooed loudly nine more times.

Crawling upstairs he heard his wife sigh out from the bedroom, 'late again Victor?'

'Yes, dear, just struck twelve, I believe.'

Gertrude McGurk turned over in her bed and added nonchalantly, 'Good God, that reminds me, I'll have to get that clock fixed tomorrow, I just heard it cuckoo three times then it said 'Oh shit,' farted loudly and cuckooed another nine times.'

BURSTING WITH HEALTH

or

Farting and Health

If you want to stay healthy and sane,
And for this I'm afraid you must train,
Scrub backside and belly,
Don't fart and be smelly,
And remember your brain not to strain.

One thing is certain, if you are already ill and short of wind, farting will not improve your condition. 2,000 years ago the Roman writer Pliny recognised this fact but then he tended to diagnose all illness as being due to anal eruptions in one way or another. Heart attacks, sore thumbs, blindness or deafness all received the same treatment:

> . . . in this disease it were better for to represse the said windiness and flatuositie.

Any similarity between Pliny and the reader's local General Practitioner is entirely intentional. For the overworked doctor there is only one thing worse than a faulty diagnosis and that is prescribing the wrong medicine. Having gone that far, the

41

bowels of a normal healthy patient will usually suffer severe shell-shock while his gut defends itself bravely against unprovoked attack from the pharmaceutical industry.

Rip Rasper in bed with a chill,
Had swallowed a massive great pill,
He said, 'When I fart
My head falls apart,
And my guts they feel terribly ill.'

In the past we were often led to believe that a leaky fundament could easily cause an early death, which is exactly what happened in the case of the Roman Emperor Claudius. Curiously enough, Claudius was of the opinion that toxic blasts from the breech actually benefitted the body physically, but this idea didn't seem to apply to himself and his destiny turned out to be a sad one. A pioneer ahead of his time, Claudius believed in the healthy freedom-loving side of farting. Sadly he died due to a ferociously fiery smacker he accidentally let himself.

His death has puzzled medical men for centuries, and opinions vary as to whether it is actually possible to die as a result of detonating via the hind-quarters. In the case of poor Claudius it was more than possible, as he suffered from high blood pressure and by all accounts having ejected an obstreperous rear-end volley would most probably have suffered a heart attack – 'death by misadventure', if you like!

Seneca, the celebrated Roman poet (normally a kindly chap), even found time after Claudius's death to maintain sarcastically:

> Typical of dearest old Claudius, he died speaking the kind of language he'd been speaking with his mouth for the vast majority of his life.

Some years ago the American doctor John Loughran published a book entitled *Ninety Days To A Better Heart* which would amply support the medical case for Claudius's untimely death. He wrote:

> A fact not generally recognised is that the heart may be subjected to great pressure from gas in the stomach. It has been found that in many instances the blood pressure becomes normal as soon as the gas is liberated. Conversely, artificial inflation of the colon with air consistently raises blood pressure. When the air is released, pressure falls . . .'

In the days of Ancient Greece and Rome the smoking of cigarettes was not as common as it is today; nowadays governments are obsessed with the health dangers associated with this anti-social habit.

Tho' smoking can cause us diseases,
Any idiot knows that, by Jesus,
Yet farting too often
Causes brain cells to soften,
And can blow our whole body to pieces!

So beware, a yawning rump can prove just as risky as smoking – but where are the 'pressure groups' amongst us in favour of advertising these dangers?

From the man who invented the diary, Samuel (What's-That-Rumpus-In-My-Bowels?) Pepys, come 'piles' of unhappy reports of a great talent unable to enjoy 'sound' health during his own lifetime:

> Today's the King's birthday – most of the day in bed, farting and colic.
>
> (*Diary*, 29 May 1665)

Like most of us, Pepys had his 'ups and downs' (in his case mostly 'downs'). Contemporaries ridiculed Pepys' frequent visits to his doctor maintaining he was the kind of man, 'who went running to the doctor if a fart lost its way in his posterior.'

'Next Please!'

Pepys often referred to his own hind-quarters as his 'farting-barrel', and is reported to have suffered 'windiness, belching and blasting of the stomach and belly'. It is said he possessed the uncanny ability to produce at will a 'thorough-cough', i.e. he could cough and break wind backwards at the same time. Unfortunately, this event was never recorded in his diary 'for posterity'.

Psychology as a branch of the health sciences was not terribly well developed in Pepys' day – which is surprising for farting has always played an important role in the psychological well-being of mankind. The embarrassment for instance, which ensues as a result of repulsive anal evacuations appals even the most ignorant amongst us – we just cannot stomach it!

The classic case of a husband returning on his birthday from work and being met by his wife at the door explains all. Inside the door the husband is blindfolded and taken into the kitchen where there are three surprises awaiting him. Having given him the first two packages his wife presumably leaves to fetch the third. Alone, he feels around to open the first package and discovers it contains a pipe, while from the second he unpacks a large bathtowel. Awaiting his wife's return, he sits down pipe in mouth and suddenly thumps out a bloodthirsty volley from his rear, the obnoxious smell of which he fans away with the large towel. His wife returns, opens the curtains and reveals the third surprise – all his work colleaques sitting silently behind him eagerly waiting for the party to begin!

Rip Rasper's right into psychology
(Often laughed at as silly mythology),
He's discovered what it means,
When we fart in our dreams,
Now I think that he's owed an apology.

46

Psychologically speaking, the golden rule is never to admit to having farted at all – even if there are only two of you present! Demonstrate your own innocence by turning up your nose at the horrible pong and complaining bitterly.

Having released a repulsive barrage, a very natural and human reaction is to seek revenge. That medieval gasbag Geoffrey Chaucer entertained the idea that revenge was moral where farting was concerned. Take the case of the flatuous Nicholas and the extremely irate Absalom:

> *This Nicholas at once let fly a fart*
> *As loud as if it were a thunder-clap.*
> *Absalom was near blinded by the blast, poor chap,*
> *But his hot iron was ready; with a thump*
> *He smote him in the middle of the rump.*

One is surprised just how gullible members of the public can be, for experience teaches us that it is unwise to have faith in every new health trend or theory appearing on the market. Our suspicion is aroused even more when we consider the sanity of the great minds who cook up these new-fangled ideas – take, for example, the celebrated founder of modern psychology himself:

Rip Rasper and some unemployeds,
Had believed in a theory of Freud's,
They took his advice
Built a farting device,
The machine has developed haemorrhoids!

For most of us, the psychological stress caused by one single fart is probably acceptable, but when the volleys just refuse to stop, the situation can become unbearable, even suicidal. Subconsciously the individual's 'seat' of thought becomes disturbed, and losing control of his senses, in'stinkt' takes over:

Rip Rasper had gone off his head,
To the doctor he had to be led.
'Psychologically speaking,
Your bunghole is leaking,
Stop farting or soon you'll be dead.'

. . . in'stinkt' takes over

Doubtless our friend Rip Rasper could have earned himself a more 'glowing' reputation. Over the years his character has been reduced to that of a psychologically depressed, irrelevant being. His name has been associated with all that is anti-social, arrogant and lazy. Why is it that a flustered or agitated person is said to be 'rushing about like a fart in a colander and doesn't know which hole to come out of'? Why do we describe a lazy individual as 'farting about'? The idea of the fart as a miser is a particularly tragic side of his character make-up. We read in the *Financial Times* of a bankrupt company where the Director is being pursued by creditors 'like the stink following a fart'.

But Rip Rasper is not all bad, and it is our duty to show more tolerance towards the fart today than ever before. The Ancient Greeks were very positive in their praise for farting and the nether regions, in general, as one famous Greek physician proved when his students were posed the following teaser:

> 'What is then the most durable and strongest part of our human body?'

Puzzled, no answer was forthcoming; then, smiling, the professor responded:

> Why, it is that part you are sitting on, dear students, for it is always cracking, but never does break.

Finally, let us finish with a useful medical warning. The consumption of tablets is not to be recommended before expelling wind from the rear – the consequences can prove tragic. Even the medical profession itself must pay attention here, for it was none other than Rip Rasper's own doctor who ended up 'breathing his last' while on holiday in Scotland:

> *Rip's doctor so fat and obese,*
> *Whose bowels would give him no peace,*
> *He closed down his practice,*
> *And the very sad fact is,*
> *He died in a Gents in Dumfries.*

For 'sound' health, read instructions carefully!

AIRS AND GRACES

or

Farting and Etiquette

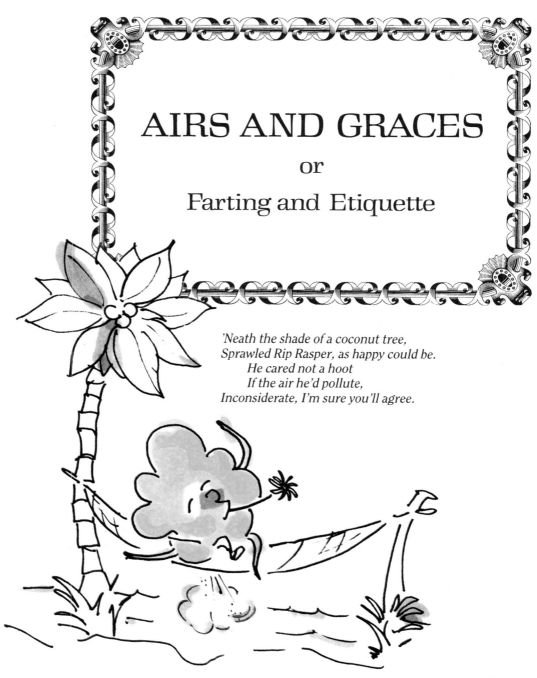

'Neath the shade of a coconut tree,
Sprawled Rip Rasper, as happy could be.
He cared not a hoot
If the air he'd pollute,
Inconsiderate, I'm sure you'll agree.

Today, after-dinner farting on a full belly with a fat cigar is no longer terribly fashionable, and unless you possess some special ability to make your 'effarts' sound vaguely musical or entertaining you can forget it! In general, provided your back-side battery is accompanied by some sort of apology, society today favours the individual with the 'guts' to let rip with gusto, rather than a cowardly attempt to 'bottle-up' the explosion inside the colon – but be careful you don't overdo it!

Rip Rasper, whilst dining at table,
Let a fart which he thought would enable
All his guests to relax,
To enjoy his wisecracks,
But instead they were rendered disabled.

Rip's Wise 'Cracks'

Again, it is difficult nowadays to conceive of a loud blasting fanfare from the rear as a welcoming or friendly gesture. In our forefathers' day however, this was often the case! Not only did a barrage from behind signify that you were well-mannered but that your aims were peaceful and that you had something of an intellectual nature to contribute.

Let's assume your bad manners have got the better of you and having ejected a monster and insulted the sense of all present, immediate refusal to accept responsibility is a typical human reaction. In fact the treatment of the rear-end as an autonomous creature followed by loud denunciation of the buttocks is sadly all too common. In many cases it is simply the volume of the emission which insults the senses most, and just how loud farts can prove to be is yet to be scientifically measured. In Celtic countries for example, tradition has placed much importance on the acoustic properties of farting with the result that time and again, hopes and expectations for loud volume rose so high that the eventual pathetic ill-mannered result proved disappointing. The situation of a vulgar northern housewife in the late 1950s was a case in point:

> *The overweight Mrs McWeir,*
> *Kept her backside blocked up for a year.*
> *When the great day arrived,*
> *She farted then cried,*
> *'Twas an offering that no one could hear.*

Hard luck Mrs McWeir! Let's be honest, how many of us get a red face when we fart alone in a room? We tend to forget our manners under such circumstances, don't we? In the bath, who really cares when he suddenly hears a raucous gurgling sound followed by the appearance of tiny bubbles on the surface of the water? No one – and certainly Rip Rasper is no exception:

> *Rip Rasper had often enquired,*
> *As he lay in his bath and perspired,*
> *'What are those small bubbles,*
> *That cause me such troubles?*
> *I'm afraid that my botty's backfired!'*

Farting alone in the bath is fine, but when we offer a rude anal remark in the presence of others, the situation sounds and smells quite different. What is it about farting that actually offends and gets up people's noses? Is it simply the volume of the explosion, is it the accompanying odour, or is it a combination of both? When it comes to volume, the well-mannered Chinese have always been particularly careful, and their maxim concerning humility in all walks of life 'sounds' as follows:

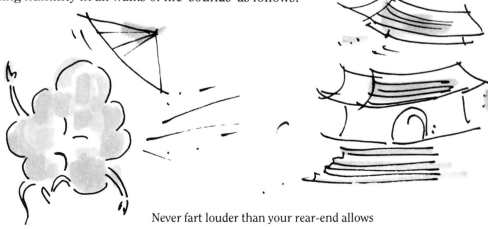

Never fart louder than your rear-end allows

54

Today scientists are generally agreed that the so-called 'Fizzle' or Shy Fart, full of complexes and produced by a confident relaxed sphincter gives off a more dangerous odour than the loud-mouthed ripping 'screamer'. This may well be the case, but intense volume also displays lack of breeding and greatly contributes towards the initial havoc and animosity associated with farting, for it bombards the senses more rapidly.

It appears what the Chinese display in the way of good manners the Scots seem to lack, for the brash pride they display in being loud farters is often outrageous, and worse still, their postern blasts are frequently carried out at their neighbour's expense:

> *A flatulent Scot named McLeod,*
> *When he farted he farted so loud,*
> *So he let go a screamer,*
> *Which destroyed most of Lima,*
> *And he sat in the wreckage so proud.*

The German Erich Maria Remarque, author of that famous novel *All Quiet On The Western Front*, obviously knew nothing about manners when it came to farting. In typical Teutonic fashion, he insisted on absolute honesty in all matters to do with venting when he rigorously pleaded:

Every little bean must be seen as well as heard

Not so well known, however, is that for a long time Remarque had been suffering from the after-effects of a strange childhood experience whilst holidaying in Spain many years before. His behaviour insulted local feeling so much that he was forced to pay 'through the nose' as a result:

> *In a street once in sunny Madrid*
> *Young Eric, was attacked by a squid,*
> *So thinking it smart,*
> *He let loose a huge fart,*
> *Was arrested and fined fifty quid.*

Intelligence proves no barrier when it comes to vulgarity. It appears great minds everywhere are prepared to travel to almost any lengths in order to create something original for the sake of 'posterity'.

> *That smelly old greek Aristotle,*
> *Was ill-mannered but awfully subtle,*
> *'I get all my ideas*
> *After guzzling ten beers,*
> *And by farting straight into the bottle!'*

Moral of the story: the 'end' justifies the means!

By the way, attempting to be too polite with regard to farting can often lead to misunderstandings and extreme embarrassment. This is often the case where no one is prepared to accept responsibility for a fart – in short, where the ownership is doubtful.

In the late 1860s Major Alexander Turnberry found himself in such a predicament. The Major had been in France visiting his acquaintance Countess de Valvoix. At the Countess's château a most illustrious company had assembled for afternoon tea. The butler announced that tea would shortly be served in the adjoining rooms and, not a man to miss his grub, the Major immediately jumped up on hearing this and offered the Countess his arm. On reaching the dining room door both stood back to let the other go through first. Misunderstandings occurring as they do, both ended up trying to squeeze through the door together. The tight squeeze resulted in a hoarse eruption from Turnberry's behind.

'Really!' cried the Countess indignantly, 'that's never happened to me before!'

'Did it happen to you?' enquired Turnberry. 'I thought it was me!'

In the previous instance the Countess was innocent, but as we all know, ladies are no beginners when it comes to farting. The writer Jonathan Swift thought that all female farting should take place in the home, and only in the home . . .

> . . . which entertainment would prove much more diverting round a tea-table than the usual one of scandal, since the sweetest harmony is allowed to proceed from the guts.

Sadly, the fair sex has decided to pay no attention to this advice and following the emancipation of women, the fart has accompanied the professional lady into her place of work where standards of etiquette have often been abused. The ensuing punishment has sometimes proved very harsh indeed:

> *A writer who lived in Fleet Street,*
> *Would fart when her colleagues she'd meet,*
> *She got sacked from* The Times,
> *For her foul stinking crimes,*
> *And they plugged up her rear with concrete.*

Not all ladies are as ill-mannered and unashamed as this, and in all fairness, the vast majority are at least more considerate than their male counterparts:

> *Fine Ladies do tend whilst sipping their tea,*
> *To foist quiet wafts on the company that be,*
> *Whilst the male of the species in guzzling his beer,*
> *Blasts them out vulgar, for all present to hear.*

Normal healthy young children are frequently to be found naïvely cross-questioning their parents on a variety of topics both pleasant and unpleasant. Should the subject prove just a little too dodgy, and no acceptable answer is forthcoming, the red-faced daddy could end up being caught with his trousers down.

Rip Rasper though, has an answer for everything:

Can children outfart their parents, Dad?

My dear child, everything is possible, but the competitive element in farting is not to be encouraged and the subject as a whole ought to be treated in a more relaxed fashion.

Society could learn a lesson from Mr Aloysius McGinty in this respect. McGinty, a modestly successful pig-farmer from the west coast of Ireland, had not attended mass for years, in fact that was the reason why Father Gilhooley visited him in the first place.

On entering McGinty's makeshift home, the priest witnessed the burly farmer and his 17 kids guzzling soup at table. Just as Father Gilhooley sat himself down, McGinty emitted the loudest fart the priest had ever heard from a layman.

Shocked, the priest picked himself up from the floor and

enquired puzzled: 'Bejasus man, are you doin' it all the time like this before your children?'

'Sure we have no rules at all around these parts Father,' replied McGinty, 'Sometimes I'll be doin' it first, and sometimes they'll have a go first!'

Why does society still look with disgust on the natural breezes which emanate from the human rump? The unsavoury odour as well as the volume of noise incurred allow the community to ostracise outraged backside blasters – and if you have a farting problem today, it is very possible you could end up leading a sad and lonely life.

> *A jet-setter set in his ways*
> *Lost all friends in a couple of days.*
> *'Twas the foul-smelling gases,*
> *Of which there were masses,*
> *As well as the din which he'd raise.*

Environmentalists have toyed with the idea of removing arch-farters from society – not a happy thought, as almost the entire population of the country would end up behind bars! In the following poem, Jonathan Swift portrays the sad plight of the fart in society, whose role has become that of a social outcast – a sad note upon which to finish . . .

> *Because I am by Nature blind,*
> *I wisely choose to walk behind;*
> *However, to avoid Disgrace,*
> *I let no Creature see my Face.*
> *My Words are few, but spoke with Sense:*
> *And yet my speaking gives Offence:*
> *Or, if to whisper I presume,*
> *The Company will fly the Room.*
> *By all the World I am oppress'd,*
> *And my Oppression gives them Rest.*

LOVESICK

or

Farting and Romance

Rip Rasper was after romance,
He'd been told that he hadn't a chance,
*   Now apart from his smell,*
*   He's as happy as hell,*
He's in love with two bull elephants!

Tradition has it that the romance of the honeymoon is over when the husband begins farting in his wife's presence. Being intimate with one's wife is fine, but one should never allow oneself to become over-familiar with her – a backside battery in bed is just not on. If it cannot be avoided, etiquette

60

teaches us at least to raise the bed-covers whilst leaning the posterior over the edge of the bed.

On no account should the example of Rip Rasper be followed:

For better? FOR WORSE!!!

In the interests of newly-married women everywhere, clergymen conducting the wedding ceremony would do well to rephrase their immortal words, perhaps along the following lines:

'Do you Mr Rattler Reynolds take Miss Clementine Clatterbox to be your lawful wedded wife – and by the way, do you fart in bed?'

If the answer is 'I do' – forget it, better safe than sorry, girls! The famous poet John Suckling expressed the same sentiments somewhat more eloquently:

> Love is the fart,
> Of every heart,
> It pains a man when 'tis kept close,
> And others doth offend when 'tis let loose.

If on the other hand the unlucky new bride only later gets 'wind' of her partner's dreadful drawbacks, her future could look anything but rosy – and she will probably live to regret not having tied the nuptial knot in her husband's bowels instead!

Needless to say if either of the romantic couple indulge in alcoholic excesses, this will undoubtedly strain the relationship. Poor behaviour of this kind was more than common in the 18th century when severe lessons in how to conduct oneself in the bedroom were not uncommon; Jonathan Swift was pretty direct about the whole affair:

> Now, Ponder well ye Parents dear,
> Forbid your Daughters guzzling Beer;
> Keep them to wholesome Food confin'd,
> Nor let them taste what causes Wind;
> And when she once has got the Art,
> She cannot help it for her Heart;
> But, out it flies, even when she meets
> Her Bridegroom in the Wedding-Sheets.

To a newly married couple, all manner of advice is useful, but should unwholesome gusts make themselves heard and smelt during the wedding reception itself, then even an optimist would not hold out much hope for the survival of that marriage.

To say that Lady Smithwick's lack of caution at the dinner table gave her fragile new husband the wrong impression, would be an understatement. The elderly Lady Smithwick suffered from severe flatulence and her silent gusts throughout the meal gave rise to the most rancid odours. As the evening wore on, the ageing bridegroom dining at her side became more and more irate, until suddenly he himself discharged a repulsively loud salvo from his own nether regions and bounded to his feet bellowing, 'Excuse me, ladies and gentlemen, but I was only trying to say out loud for everyone's benefit what my dear wife Lady Smithwick has been whispering to me privately all evening!'

As even the most unromantic amongst us must agree, breaking wind backwards in any company causes problems, but when it starts to interfere with happy married bliss then the joke is no longer a funny one – as Rip Rasper's cleaning lady Mrs Dixon would assure us:

A young lady from Bradford called Dixon,
Whose husband had got an affliction,
He smelt like a horse,
So she sought a divorce,
'Twas his behind that she said needed fixin'.

In the 18th century many ladies believed it romantic to suppress their back-firing at all costs, and the reports at the time show that this was not an easy task as the ill consequences of suppression could cause

Cholics, hysterics, rumbling belching spleen etc, but in women of a more strong constitution, it vents itself entirely in talkativeness.

Even today, in order to avoid embarrassment, some young ladies refuse to fart at all in their husband's presence. Sometimes the action cannot be avoided as in the case of a young London secretary invited out for the first time one evening to the cinema by her handsome new boss.

Nervously awaiting his arrival to collect her, the doorbell finally rings and she just manages to suppress a mighty eruption from her intenstines. Feeling very uneasy she opens the door and is escorted to the front seat of his huge Mercedes. Slamming her door, he disappears for a moment to make a hasty telephone call. In his absence she feels potential disaster welling up again inside her gut, and rolling over on her side she releases a passionate little breeze, giggles and feels relieved. Just then her friend returns and climbs into the driving seat.

Slightly embarrassed at forgetting his manners, he apologetically stammers, 'Jane, please forgive me, I forgot to introduce my parents.' Turning round he points to an elderly couple smiling smugly in the rear seat . . .

As it turned out young Jane avoided becoming permanently attached to her boss; alas the young lady in the following escapade was not so lucky and lived to regret her unfortunate decision:

A girl who got married from Wales,
Had the wind taken out of her sails,
The first week she enjoyed
Then her life was destroyed
By her husband's rip-roaring foul gales!

A sad 'tail', but thank God romance and . . . dammit . . . downright old-fashioned humanity is still with us:

Madam, my soul speaks when my mouth knows the moment is too divine for words

Now sexy young Rip took a chance,
To impress and to make some advance,
With the girls nauseated,
By the smell he'd created,
He then proved that he just couldn't dance.

Such embarrassing situations are not just the unhappy lot of a mere Rip Rasper, oh no! One activity ladies simply refuse to tolerate is the male of the species evacuating from the lumbar regions in public and at their expense. It does not matter how famous or talented the culprit happens to be, he need only unload one musty whiff and he is finished:

At a party once, old Fred Astaire,
After dancing forgot to take care
When he sat down he farted,
All the nice girls departed,
He's never danced since, he don't care.

At the risk of sounding unromantic, it is painful to admit that the fair sex indulge in more than their fair share of back-side blowing, and it is not just elderly, or ugly females who are responsible, but attractive young damsels also, and French

65

damsels at that! As usual we find the culprits in the ranks of the most royal, at the court of Louis XIV at Versailles – where a lot of time was spent farting about anyway.

One lusty old duke who had a way with the ladies, lay sprawled out on his deathbed surrounded by agitated young females waiting anxiously for the old lad to launch himself into eternity. Fate, however, had other things in store, for no way was the horny octogenarian going to depart without witnessing a final rallying bang. Suddenly his favourite mistress ejected a bloodthirsty cracker loud enough to 'waken the dead' – precisely the embarrassing situation the red-faced damsel had been trying to avoid all evening.

Realising what she had done, the old duke sighed painfully, pathetically turned his head to his most beloved and gasped, 'Anastasia, Anastasia, I'm dying and you speak of love!'

We have to accept the fact; however; that women are not nearly as embarrassed by farting as men would like to believe and the classic case of the romantic young couple in love strolling up the steep hill bears this out. Nearing the top, the boy suddenly whiffed a foul odour, and, flushed with embarrassment, asked the girl whether she had farted:

Gallup polls carried out by some of the more popular women's magazines indicate that shy retiring widows around 45–50 years old, 'under pressure' at work or elsewhere, are the main culprits when it comes to secreting romantic rear-end fragrance:

> *Now widows, they say are not shy,*
> *But poor Aggie she wanted to die,*
> *Well she'd blast with great ease,*
> *Which the men did not please,*
> *For she smelt like a pig in a sty.*

At last the day seems to have dawned when the emancipated male of the species no longer requires to conceal his blushing red cheeks when out pushing his child in the pram – or are there some of us left who still need to be emancipated . . .?

> *Rip Rasper whilst walking the kiddy,*
> *Felt his brain gettin' kindoffa giddy,*
> *All the people who passed,*
> *Would giggle and ask,*
> *'He did it again then Rip, did he?'*

Rip Rasper is not the only adult male to suffer embarrassment as a result of a seething infantile backside, but let's be honest, lads, the ladies seem better able to cope with the whole situation than us men. Nevertheless, to say women never get embarrassed whenever their own botties scream for help would be simply untrue.

A choosy fat lady was purchasing an expensive Persian carpet in a well-known London store when she bent double to feel the texture. Suddenly she exploded from behind with two yelping thuds which resounded throughout the entire saleroom. Apologising and blushing profusely, she straightened up and looked more than uncomfortable. The small exasperated salesman behind her smiled wryly, adding, 'Not to worry, Madam, I'll be expecting much worse when I tell you the price!'

The motto of the story is that women will literally 'stoop to anything' – even to fart. The more you blast young men, the more romantic women will find you . . . so get on with it and start romancing!

ARTY FARTY

or

Farting and the Arts

An artist who thought he was smart,
Cast a sculpture which looked like a fart.
Every day he'd appear,
And the public would jeer,
'Is that what you classify art?'

RIP RASPER

For over 2,000 years man has been trying to render the sensitive subject of farting more palatable to the noses of the public. Historians, musicians and artists of the highest calibre, all have attempted to describe or depict in some manner or other the phenomenon of the fart; even Rip Rasper has tried his hand – with disastrous results:

Friends, Romans, countrymen,
Lend me your REARS!

Shakespeare turned out to be a real 'gas' on the subject of breaking wind and it is a pity that today we cannot treat farting and Shakespeare with the humour they both deserve. Shakespeare even allowed his hero Hamlet to fart twice, but being a

'Reading one's own poetry is like smelling one's own farts.'
W.H.Auden

bit of a coward, Shakespeare preferred to use the words 'buz-buz' instead of 'fart' (Act 2, scene 2).

Certainly our former poet laureate was not as squeamish in expressing himself as Billy Shakespeare turned out to be.

When it comes to literature and farting, La Belle France has produced more 'material' than most other countries put together, for example the humorous little pamphlet published in 1540 called *Le Plaisant deuis du Pet,* a story about an unhappy wife who cannot stop farting. Various medical books such as *Physiologia Crepitus Ventris,* published in 1607, also crept on to the market and proved popular, at least amongst 'Pharting-Physicians'.

But the absolute star prize in the world of farting literature must go to the 1200-page *Bible of Farting* written in 1628; it served as the basis for all future offerings on the subject. Plays to do with farting, however, are a very rare commodity indeed; nevertheless, in 1750 the playwright Polichinel produced a 'Five Act Farting Tragedy' where each 'Act' consisted of one massive riproaring volley from the actor's back-passage! No mercy was shown as the audience erupted hysterically.

'A Five Act Farting Tragedy' starring Rip Rasper.

This list of fart-literature is by no means 'exhaustive'. Interestingly enough, the only real contribution in the English langauge consists of a meagre 16-page booklet published in 1722 entitled *The Benefit of Farting Explained.* It contains an article

THE BENEFIT OF

FARTING

EXPLAINED:

OR,

THE FUNDAMENT-ALL CAUSE

OF THE

DISTEMPERS INCIDENT TO THE FAIR SEX,

INQUIRED INTO:

PROVING À POSTERIORI MOST OF THE DISORDURES IN-TAILED
ON THEM ARE OWING TO FLATULENCIES NOT
SEASONABLY VENTED.

Wrote in Spanish, by Don *Fart-in-hando Puff-indorst*, Professor
of *Bum-bast* in the University of Craccow:

AND

Translated into English, at the request and for the use of the
Lady *Damp-fart*, of *Her-fart-shire.*

BY OBADIAH FIZLE,

GROOM OF THE STOOL TO THE PRINCESS OF ARS-MINI IN
SARDINIA.

The SIXTH EDITION, revised by a College of
Fizz-icians.

LONDON:

PRINTED FOR A. MOORE, NEAR ST PAUL'S, AND SOLD BY
THE BOOKSELLERS.

1722.

Title page of the only real 'offering' on the subject of farting in English.

on the advantage of anal conversation as well as comments on the more dire consequences which result from over-indulgence.

A few centuries later and probably to make up for this poor recognition of the fart in the English language, James Joyce offers us the longest single sentence in the history of not just English, but all human literature. At the 'back' of this 'long-winded' literary offensive is, of course, our friend the fart – who else? The 'hole' effort takes up some 60 pages of his mammoth volume *Ulysses* and comprises a masterful soliloquy performed by Molly Bloom squatted on a chamber-pot – farting all the while.

Indeed, *Ulysses* is full of anal gusts from start to finish and this should come as no surprise when we consider the musical pedigree of its bespectacled author:

That writer from Ireland named Joyce,
Who sang with such sweetness of voice,
He would often just poop,
Before starting a book,
And produce the most horrible noise.

Rasper's Wind Symphony No. 9

Talking of noises both horrible and pleasant, almost all of us have to admit an almost infantile interest in the varied sounds that accompany our breaking wind backwards. This interest in the musical side of farting is nothing new.

Centuries ago, a French surgeon named Jerome Carden undertook a musical study of the fart to investigate its tonal qualities and sound possibilities. Carden distinguished four key-notes – 'fundamental' notes, if you like, together with 58 variations. In other words, it was theoretically possible for a human being to produce 62 different notes providing his posterior was 'in tune'.

73

Jonathan Swift, scribbling away at the beginning of the 18th century, spent a lot of time analysing the progress of musical theory and here's what he managed to 'drum' up:

> The first discovery of harmony was owing to an observation of persons of different sizes sounding different notes in music, by farting; by this rule it would be an easy matter to form a farting concert, by ranging persons of different sizes in order, as you would a ring of bells, or a set of organ pipes.

On the stage as he ate Tortellini
Rip emptied a glass of Martini
He blasted with vigour,
And without even a snigger,
Maintained 'twas composed by Puccini.

One of the greatest musical geniuses of all time, old 'piggy-wiggy' Mozart certainly did his fair share of *fortissimo* farting particularly when he was young. What's more he wasn't always willing to own up to his filthy deeds. In a letter to his mother in Mannheim written in January 1778 he seemed happy to report that he had composed nothing at all for an entire week and admitted he was more interested in discussing farts – which is exactly what he did for the remainder of the letter:

74

At night of farts there is no lack,
Which are let off, forsooth, with a powerful crack,
The king of farts came yesterday
Whose farts smelt sweeter than they may.

Through these and similar letters, we begin to witness the other side of Mozart's character – the backside!

But it was not just Teutonic composers who spent their spare time 'farting about', for in the prudest corner of old Britannia Rip Rasper was also 'blowing his horn' only this time Rip's 'Slow Movement' backfired and he was left to face the music alone:

Rip Rasper his friends to regale,
Used to fart in F-sharp in a pail,
*   But those sweet smelling songs,*
*   Produced foul putrid pongs,*
Which earned him six months in the jail.

No prizes for Rip's poisonous rear-end orchestrations here, I'm afraid!

Prizes, however, should be handed out to the hero in the next episode. The M.Fa. or Master of Farts degree in the musical world must go to a young, recently deceased musician from Greece. Sadly, breathtaking musical ability and excessive competitive spirit could not prevent the tragic termination of a career in its prime. The following few verses pay tribute to the outstanding musical contribution made by the late 'Farter from Sparta'.

THE FARTER FROM SPARTA

There was a young fellow from Sparta
A really magnificent farter,
    On the strength of one bean
    He'd fart God Save the Queen
And Beethoven's Moonlight Sonata.

He could vary, with proper persuasion
His fart to suit any occasion,
    He could fart like a flute
    Like a lark, like a lute,
This highly fartistic Caucasian.

This sparkling young farter from Sparta,
His fart for no money would barter.
    He could roar from his rear
    Any scene from Shakespeare,
Whilst he chewed on an old chipolata.

He'd fart a gavotte for a starter
And frizzle a fine serenata.
    He could play on his anus
    The Coriolanus:
Tum-titty, tum-titty, tum tatta.

He was great in the Christmas Cantata,
He could double-stop fart the Toccata,
    He'd boom from his ass
    Bach's B-Minor Mass
And in counterpoint, La Traviata.

His basso profundo with timbre so rare,
He rendered quite often, with power to spare.
    But his great work of art,
    His fortissimo fart,
He saved for the Marche Militaire.

His repertoire ranged from classics to jazz,
He achieved new effects with bubbles of . . .
    With a good dose of salts
    He could whistle a waltz
Or swing it in razzamatazz.

One day he was dared to perform
The William Tell Overture Storm,
    But naught could dishearten
    Our spirited Spartan,
For his fart was in wonderful form.

It went off in capital style,
And he farted it through with a smile.
    Then feeling quite jolly
    He tried the finale,
Blowing double-stopped farts all the while.

The selection was tough, I admit,
But it did not dismay him one bit,
    Then, with ass thrown aloft
    He suddenly coughed. . . .
And collapsed in a shower of shit.

His bunghole was blown back to Sparta,
Where they buried the rest of our farter
    With a gravestone of turds
    Inscribed with the words:
'To the Fine Art of Farting, a Martyr.'

The visual arts have also earned themselves a place in the 'Farting Hall of Fame', and the paintings of Brueghel or Hieronymus Bosch depicting medieval 'bean-feasts' of gluttony and debauchery are full of individuals given over to the emission of bubbling hurricanes from their rear.

Nor should we turn a blind eye (or deaf ear) to the artists of today, many of whom are no less productive than their predecessors. That magnificent exponent of the Surrealist school Salvador Dali, for example, churned out canvases at a tremendous rate for years 'on end' – in fact he seemed to have got it down to a 'fine art':

> That painter called Salvador Dali,
> Exhibiting once in Somali,
>   To express his fine art,
>   At the canvas he'd fart,
> 'In this job you don't shilly-shally'.

78

Dali amassed a vast monetary fortune and ended up 'stinking rich'. Not so with another talented artist who proved every bit as powerful when it came to blasting out violent reprimands with his rump – in fact Henry ruined so many pairs of trousers in this way, he could no longer afford to dress himself properly:

> That crepitant sculptor called Moore,
> Great handicaps had to endure,
> Whilst working with bronze,
> He'd wear nowt but long-johns,
> To buy trousers the man was too poor.

Another painter who was not at all squeamish about blowing either his top (or his bottom) was the German painter Albrecht Dürer. No slouch with the old paint-box, Dürer was on the scene shouting his mouth off even before Shakespeare was undergoing major surgery for nappy-rash. As a student in his sick-bed, Dürer knew how good his talents were and disrespectfully decided to let his mentors know just that:

> Albrecht Dürer while still in a coma,
> Let a fart of such fetid aroma
> His professor took fright
> As his student turned white
> But he still got a first class Diploma!

So the fart is a permanent force to be reckoned with in artistic circles and his *forte* lies in the fact that he is not re-'tailed' as a fashionable commodity, rather he seems to have developed a lasting 'deep-seated' appeal of his own. He is being written and talked about today just as fervently and lovingly as he was 2,000 years ago!

Congratulations, Rip Rasper!

INTERNATIONAL TENSION
or Farting and Nationality

An old Scottish fart called McCrumpett,
Was renowned for the blowing of his trumpet,
He'd lift up his kilt
An old tune he would lilt,
Saying, 'There's music noo, like it or lump it!'

According to history, southern peoples are better able to produce greater amounts of foul gas than their northern counterparts. Knowing how southerners respect their garlic, onions, figs and sweet wines there may be some truth in this statement. Of course, not all nations are as prudish about farting as the British. The only real publication on the subject in English appeared in the 18th century and sold little more than 50 copies. France, the classic land of farting, was not impressed.

The French language, it seems, is better suited to providing picturesque descriptions of the fine art of bowel-trumpeting. What other language can boast such classy offerings as 'ouvrir la tabernacle' (Open your tabernacle) or 'ouvrir la tabatière' (Open your snuffbox)? Unfortunately Rip Rasper almost 'snuffed it' himself upon opening his own snuff-box:

Open Your Snuffbox

Two of the longest farting nations in all history, the Romans and the Greeks, regarded farting as so important that they actually invented special names for certain types of emission, the loud cracking *Crepitus* (Greek: *Porde*) and the silent sneaky offering, the *Flatus*, (Greek: *Psophos*).

The word *Flatus* has given our language the term 'inflation', the similarity being clear, both *Flatus* and 'inflation' are sneaky things that stink to high heaven!

The Spaniards followed suit and had their *Pedo Fuerte* and *Pedo Suave*, but just exactly which of the two Picasso used in the execution of the following painting is open to question:

That baldy old artist Picasso,
Would polish his rear-end with brasso,
With colours so smart
A still-life he would fart,
And it hangs to this day in El Paso.

What about the Orient? The Japs and Koreans seem to take little offence at being reprimanded by their neighbour's backside. The Chinese are similar and refuse to take seriously anything which, to use their own expression, 'drifts from the valley of the wines.'

Is it true that all folk Japanese,
Tend to fart really loud when they sneeze?
Is it true Hirohito,
Had some tests incognito,
'Cos he thought he'd caught some strange disease?

So it seems some nations are more apprehensive about letting-rip than others, but in western Europe the Irish seem to be one of the few nations prepared to put their money where their hind-quarters are, plumping for a diet of cabbage and Guinness – a recipe guaranteed to produce dry-rot in the bowel.

But the Irish, being not just great farters but practical people as well, have at least attempted to put their farting ability to good use in solving their country's problems. Professor O'Toole, the smart Dublin academic, appeared to have all the answers:

That economist Breecher O'Toole,
For farting developed a new rule,
'If your land's in a mess,
Vent more and not less.'
He made men like Karl Marx look a fool!

North of the border, from the land that gave us whisky and haemorrhoids, Jock is prepared to bet his 'bottom' twopenny piece on a consommé made from boiled corks and castor oil, which would certainly not outdo a badly cooked haggis! A common phrase for a fart in the 18th century was a 'Scotch warming pan', probably alluding to the fact that the Scots were

82

capable of extracting and re-using the heat contained in such a detonation; certainly Rip Rasper was not the only one to be impressed by such thriftiness!

A SCOTSMAN'S NO' HAPPY UNTIL HE GETS MORE,
FROM ONE SINGLE FART, HE'LL PRODUCE FOUR !!

Farting is an art at which Yugoslavians seem to excel. Years ago an elderly villager in the west of the country had become notorious for his ability to make fools of the village youth.

'Hurry, I've an urgent message to be delivered. Who can run the fastest?' he bellowed one morning, challenging a group of loud boisterous teenagers standing near him.

Sensing the chance of a quick dinar, the strongest of the group forced his way forward at the others' expense, 'Me, it's me,' he screamed.

The old man beckoned him to come closer, and with the boy standing almost on top of him, Grandpa raised his feeble leg and let rip a screeching toxic thunderbolt. 'Get your skates on, lad, and overtake that one,' he chuckled happily.

To give credit where it's due, the French are the only people to have classified the fart according to sex, dividing 'him' up into various categories depending on his own odiferous qualities. In the female fart section, for example, are to be found the Young Lady's Fart, the Married Woman's Fart, the Virgin's Fart etc. Then come the professional classification the Seamstress's Fart, the Nun's Fart and so it continues. Amongst the male of the species are included the Brewer's Fart and the Baker's Fart. Eventually we reach tonal classifications with examples such as the Muffled Fart or the Whispering Fart.

'Wind' and weather permitting, the flatulent French thinker Descartes wrestled for years with the subject of farting, and every schoolboy is familiar with his famous maxim – 'I think, therefore I fart.' Nevertheless, M. Descartes was unable, it seems, to get to the 'bottom' of the following query concerning Rip Rasper's bowel-philosophy:

> *Rip Rasper, who'd studied Descartes,*
> *Was as usual trying to be smart.*
> *'Since I think, I exist,*
> *(Which I don't when I'm pissed)*
> *But what does it mean when I fart?'*

When it comes to laughs, the subject of farting is as internationally acceptable as any other branch of humour. There is no

84

country on earth where people's feelings have not been aroused by the statements made by their own or other people's backsides.

The following list bears witness to the international success enjoyed by our fetid friend Rip Rasper down through the centuries:

Old Norse	freta
Anglo-Saxon	feortan
Old-English	feorten
Old High German	furten
Sanskrit	pard
Lithuanian	perdzu
Spanish	pédo
Norwegian	fise
Swedish	fjärt
Icelandic	freta
Hungarian	fzellelpés
Portuguese	traque
Finnish	pieru
Irish	bram
Turkish	vellenm
Polish	pierdzenie
Japanese	onara
Korean	bang gu
Czech	psoŭk
Dutch	windje
Italian	peto
Danish	fis
French	pet

~~I FART, THEREFORE I WAS~~

~~I AM, THEREFORE I FART~~

I FART, THEREFORE I AM!!

Compared to us Westerners, our Eastern bloc neighbours are required to be that bit more thrifty and inventive in order to make 'ends' meet. In most Eastern households at the moment, the fart is used solely as a means of warming the bed and no substantial contribution is made by it, for example, to improving orthodox heating habits. Recent experiments in the Soviet Union aim to change this state of affairs as the fart is examined

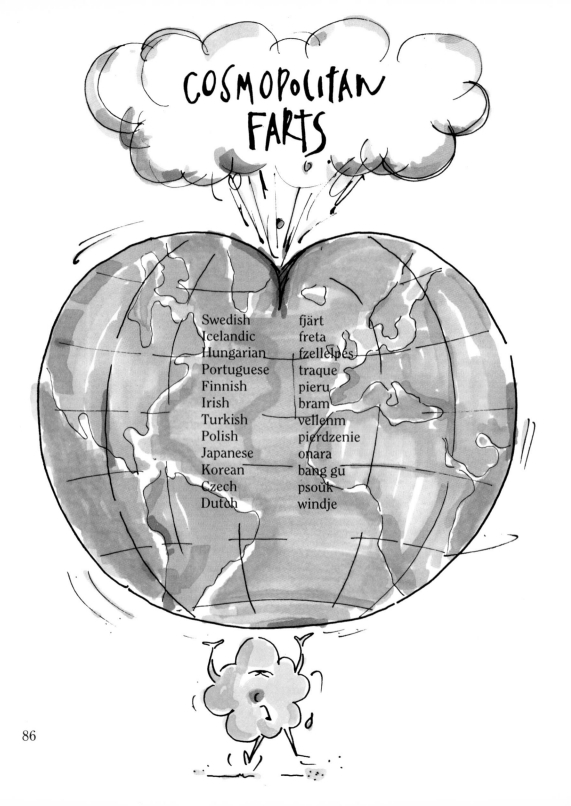

COSMOPOLITAN FARTS

Swedish	fjärt
Icelandic	freta
Hungarian	fzellelpes
Portuguese	traque
Finnish	pieru
Irish	bram
Turkish	vellenm
Polish	pierdzenie
Japanese	onara
Korean	bang gu
Czech	psouk
Dutch	windje

in the context of a 'National Heating Code'. Under the socialist system, all citizens are encouraged to take part in the 'Fart More and Heat the Country' campaign, much to the amusement of Westerners and Americans alike.

Increasing Natural Output – Soviet style!

But the superpowers have not just been waging a COLD war about who should have the right to HEAT the world properly. It seems that the energy the Soviets are prepared to put into their National Heating Programmes, the Americans invest in the Space Race. Determining who in future centuries shall have the right to blast heavenly perfumes in outer space is, let's face it, nothing to turn one's nose up at – after all, which nation today would not be 'over the moon' were it able to proclaim proudly:

It's one small gust for man,
And one giant blast for mankind.

Sceptical 'arse'-tronauts like RipRasper, however, still maintain that mankind is not profiting sufficiently from the vast technological advances being made as a result of the Space Race:

'Twas technology sent Rip to the moon,
An event which proved him no goon,
But what use is being smart,
When he can't stop a fart,
From going off in his own pantaloons?

Still, Uncle Sam will really have to excel himself in order to live up to the reputation of the gassiest Soviet citizen of all time, the Volga Boatman, who, in his own humble way and when on form could prove very very 'volga' indeed! 'Yo – ho – heave – ho –'

All said and done, for sheer professionalism the French must go top of the international farting league – but they don't have it all their own way. Although they slurp tremendous quantities of wine, some observers maintain the 'sweet smell' of success has still somehow eluded that unhappy and explosive nation:

Why is it those people, the French,
After boozing their thirst for to quench,
When it comes to the fart
They can't manage the art,
Of getting it right with the stench?

Quel désastre terrible!!!

A MASTER OF FARTS
or The Greatest Farter of All Time

The farts of Pujol they'd adore,
In that theatre they called Pompadour,
At the candles he'd shoot,
Or blow trills on his flute,
By using his rear embouchure.

Author's Note: The author apologises for interruptions made by Rip Rasper throughout this chapter due to reasons beyond his control. (Downright jealousy!)

In this final chapter, Rip Rasper must be content to share the stage with a veritable genius, in fact with a specimen unique in the history of world farting. Up until his death in 1945 Josef Pujol, better known as 'Le Petomane', was to become the greatest and most talented farter the world had ever known. Growling away on stage on a good night he earned more money than most of the leading popular singers of the day – including Sarah Bernhardt and Yvette Guilbert! The man was a medical phenomenon and an artistic genius of the highest calibre. That unforgettable singer Guilbert wrote:

> They fell over themselves to hear him and the laughter, shouting, women's shrieking and the whole hysterical din could be heard a hundred yards away from the Moulin Rouge. That Sunday, Le Petomane's takings were 1,000 louis!

Nicknamed 'the only artist who pays no author's royalties', it was whilst still a boy that Pujol realised he had been chosen by God to fulfil a very special role in life. Bathing with his chums on the Marseilles beaches one day, he realised he had unconsciously inhaled water through his behind without intending to do so. Visits to the local doctor saw his 'illness' dismissed as a childish joke. Some joke!

Whilst playing one day on the beach,
Little Joe let one helluva screech,
Looking down to the ground,
He heard an odd sound,
As the seawater entered his breech!

Later, during military service, Pujol received continued encouragement from his friends who advocated he should try to make a living using his 'unusual ability'. No stranger to the stage, Pujol thought the risk worth taking, and opened a small theatre in Marseilles which met with instant success. After touring the provincial towns of the south in 1892, Pujol at last headed for the big one, for Paris.

He was signed up immediately by the Moulin Rouge and became an overnight success. Dressed in his elegant costume, red coat and with red silk collar, black satin breeches to the knees, black stockings and patent leather shoes, he added the final touch by donning bow-tie and white gloves, cane and top-hat. He looked exquisite, and night after night succeeded in astounding the delighted audiences with his highly amusing PETOMANE SHOW – although one individual who shall remain anonymous was not at all in agreement with the success the maestro was enjoying:

Jealousy will get you everywhere!

Before each performance the maestro would explain that he had the power to breathe in air via his anus just as members of the audience could breathe in through their mouths. Using this body of air contained in his intestines, he could reproduce at will all sorts of sounds. Turning his back, he then proceeded with his famous 'Catalogue of Farts – the Mother-in-Law's Fart, the Bride-on-Her-Wedding-Night's Fart (quiet and short), then the morning after (very loud), the Mason's Fart.

'This one's a dressmaker ripping two yards of calico' – a fart which lasted at least 10 seconds and imitated the sound of material being torn to shreds. Rapturous applause.

Disappearing behind the curtain for a moment, he would re-appear with a tube about a yard long, one end inserted into his body and in other a lighted cigarette. The contraction of the muscles allowed the cigarette to be 'smoked' and the smoke subsequently 'blown' out. His next trick was to remove the cigarette and replace it with a small flute upon which he proceeded to play 'Au Clair de la Lune'.

The dramatic finale followed when he turned round and extinguished the gas jets of the footlights with tremendous force and panache. If the audience was fit enough after all the laughing to join him for a final song, then that's what normally happened. It was common during each performance for at least three or four spectators – normally ladies, to faint as a result of over-laughing.

People also fainted during his more daring and dangerous private performances where his tricks included lowering himself into a basin full of water, sucking up water by contraction of the muscles and blasting out a silver-tongued cadence via his rump. This tremendous stunt succeeded in impressing even the most arrogant sceptics amongst the audience – except of course one – Rip Rasper:

Anything he can do I can do better . . .

King Leopold II of Belgium visited one of these private performances incognito, and shoved 20 francs into his hand after the show.

> Oh the screams and the shouts and the laughter,
> As he'd let out another great wafter,
> With a beautiful tune,
> On rear-end bassoon,
> The audience got dafter and dafter.

All were united in laughing at Pujol's genius, and success continued as he 'unloaded' his talents in Belgium, Spain and most of North Africa. In 1895 after continual developments to his act, he 'turned his back' on the Moulin Rouge and opened his own theatre, the Théâtre Pompadour. With the help of his children singing and dancing on stage, he himself was still top of the bill with a show which included many new exotic animal imitations.

Although happy and unbelievably successful, Pujol allowed himself to become involved in a serious legal wrangle with his former employer, the Moulin Rouge. The battle lasted six years and is definitely the longest legal case involving farting on record! Because he had performed at the market-stall of a friend for nothing, he was sued for 'breech' of contract and fined 3,000 francs. Pujol, intent on getting his own back on the Moulin Rouge, heard they had employed Angele Thiebeau, a female petomane to take over his old job. The 'Phoney Farter' as she was called, really was a fake; she performed with a bellows under her skirt!

Pujol intended to sue for fraudulent imitation and counterfeit, but on 13 March 1898 he was beaten to it by the newspaper *L'Art Lyrique et le Music Hall*. The paper pronounced the female petomane to be a fake and within 24 hours her name was mud in the Paris farting scene. Her career lay in ruins and she was left to pick up the pieces (and her bellows).

Pujol was happy, justice had been done. As the manager of the Black Cat Nightclub, next door to the Moulin Rouge, commented at the time: 'Pujol was a good workman from the "bottom" up!'

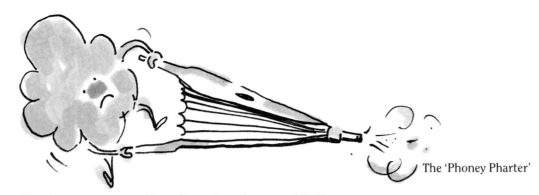

The 'Phoney Pharter'

Pujol's success continued unabated up until the war years started making life difficult for him. The family could no longer help out on stage and finally in 1918 the Théâtre Pompadour closed for the last time. Le Petomane returned to his old job as a baker and lived on until 1945 when he died, having farted his last at the ripe old age of 88.

Hearing of his death, the University's Faculty of Medicine immediately offered 25,000 francs for the right to examine his corpse. Thank God the family refused permission, for like Humpty Dumpty, they may never have been able to put him back together again!

With the maestro dead and gone, it seems rather late and inappropriate to entertain a hypocrite. Sadly, Rip Rasper shall have to dry his own crocodile tears.
(Insert no.116)

> *A crowd of these medical twits,*
> *Tried to cut the great Pujol to bits,*
> *All the parts from his bowels,*
> *That were causing the growls,*
> *Were arranged so that nothing else fits.*

Medical examinations had, in fact, been carried out on the maestro during his lifetime and the results published in various learned journals. For example on 27 March 1892 in the *Journal de Médecine Bordeaux* an article appeared concerning his case entitled 'The Absorption and Expulsion at Will of Air and Liquid by the Rectum'.

The most famous article concerning his medical condition appeared that same year and bore the title 'An Extraordinary Case of Rectal Breathing and Musical Anus', penned by Dr